The fantastically feminist (and totally true) story of the

INSPIRATIONAL ACTIVIST AND CAMPAIGNER

MICHELLE OBAMA

ANNA DohERty

wren & rook

MEET MICHELLE'S Family

Fraser C. Robinson
1935 – 1991

Fraser works at the Chicago water plant. He is quite ill and has trouble walking so he has to use a cane. Even though he struggles he never, ever calls in sick to work! Michelle inherits his never-give-up attitude.

Craig
1962 – Now

A superstar basketball coach. He's the absolute best big brother to Michelle, always looking after her and making her laugh.

Bo
2008 – Now

Sunny
2012 – Now

1969

Michelle lives in Chicago, USA, in a tiny one bedroom apartment with her mum, dad and brother Craig. Her parents put up a thin partition dividing the living room in two, turning it into Craig and Michelle's bedrooms.

Michelle adores spending time with
her family, playing Monopoly, reading,
listening to music, and most of all
practising piano … in fact, she
loves playing piano so much that
her parents have to remind
her to take breaks!

1970

Michelle starts school. She loves learning and is so clever that she skips her second year! Her school is very close to her house, so Michelle and her girl pals trot home to chatter about school gossip to Marian at lunchtimes.

1978

Michelle's high school is over an hour away from where she lives. She travels there every day through the noisy, busy city without complaining because she is set on doing well and going to a top university. She works the absolute hardest she can and graduates second highest in her class!

When she's not working super-hard on her homework, Michelle joins in as many activities as she can. She sings in the choir, takes dance classes and is even school treasurer.

BALLET 50

JAZZ

HOMEWORK

CHOIR

TREASURER

SCHOOL

BUS STOP

CHICAGO BUS

1981

Michelle decides she wants to go to Princeton University. Her teachers aren't sure if she has what it takes (Princeton is a very famous school for super-clever people), but Michelle works extremely hard, and is accepted as a student!

When she arrives, Michelle feels a little out of place because most of the other students and teachers are white. She helps to set up an after-school club for children of colour. She loves playing piano for the little kids.

1985

Once she graduates from Princeton, there's no stopping Michelle. She starts studying law at Harvard – another brilliant university – and joins protests demanding that Harvard take more students and teachers of colour.

1988-1989

After university, Michelle begins a new job as a lawyer in Chicago. She stands out because there are not many other female lawyers, and very few African American female lawyers!

Soon she is put in charge of looking after another student from Harvard called Barack. He thinks Michelle is wonderful! Barack keeps asking her out on a date, but Michelle always says no because they work together.

ICE CREAM

They become good friends and as she gets to know Barack better, Michelle begins to think he has a cute smile …

On the way home from an office picnic, Barack suggests they get some ice cream. Sitting on the pavement, eating chocolate ice cream (Michelle's absolute favourite flavour), they finally fall in love.

2001

Michelle and Barack have two daughters: Malia
and Sasha. Michelle teaches her girls that if they
work hard, they can achieve anything they put
their minds to! She wants them to be unafraid
of making mistakes.

2007

Barack decides to run for President of the United
States. Michelle helps him as much as she can and
they work as a team. The campaign is very exciting
because there has never been an African
American President before.

2008

Barack is voted President! He gets more votes than any other President in history. To celebrate, he and Michelle go to ten different fabulous, fancy balls on the night Barack is sworn in! How exhausting.

2008

Michelle, Barack, Malia and Sasha move into the White House in Washington DC, which is where all Presidents and their families live. Michelle is now called The First Lady (because she's married to a President). Barack is elected to be President twice in a row, which means the family will live in the White House for eight years.

The White House is enormous, with 132 rooms including a gym, bowling alley, home cinema and swimming pool! There are hundreds of staff and secret service agents in the house to look after the family and keep them safe.

The Obamas all have
secret service
code names.

Barack
Renegade

Malia
Radiance

Sasha
Rosebud

Michelle
Renaissance

Even though they are surrounded by lots of people, the Obamas try to have a normal family life. They eat dinner together, play with their dogs, have sleepovers and do homework.

Family is very important to Michelle – she even invites her own mum to come and live with them!

Michelle hangs up a painting called Resurrection (1966) by Alma Thomas. It's the first painting by an African American woman to be hung in the White House.

As the First Lady of the United States, Michelle gives up a lot of her time to fight for things she believes in. She is passionate about education, fitness and health, volunteer work, equality and women's rights.

Even though they've got their hands full running the country, she and Barack make time to volunteer in soup kitchens and homeless shelters.

Michelle spends a lot of her time travelling around the country, making speeches, talking to children and young people, and appearing on television shows to reach out to as many people as possible. She is never afraid to be silly, to sing, dance, or act out funny scenes to draw attention to something she cares about. People listen to what she has to say because she is funny, kind, clever and passionate!

2009

Michelle invites school children to help her plant an organic vegetable garden in the grounds of the White House! The food will be used to make meals in the White House, but also will be sent to local soup kitchens and food banks.

All sorts of things are grown in Michelle's garden: lettuce, spinach, onions, tomatoes, corn, broccoli, herbs, peas, carrots, cauliflower, peppers, sea kale, oats, peanuts, pumpkins, papaya, figs, squash ... There are also flowers and beehives!

2015

Michelle campaigns very hard to inspire young people to stay in education after they finish school, because she believes this is absolutely the best way to follow your dreams!

She finds out that across the world, millions of girls are not in school.

Maybe they can't afford to go, maybe the country they live in doesn't think girls need to go to school, maybe they have to stay at home to do chores, or maybe they are expected to start their own family at a very young age. Whatever the reason, Michelle thinks this is very unfair and will not rest until she does something about it ...

Michelle begins a campaign called Let Girls Learn which teaches families, world leaders and girls themselves about why going to school is important and great! It also offers help to families so girls can afford to go to school and raises money for school bathrooms and buses.

Michelle visits schools in countries all over the world and tries to help as many girls as possible.

FOLLOW YO
DREAM

2017

Even when Barack is no longer President, there's no stopping Michelle from trying to help people, especially girls! Together with Barack, she continues her campaign to keep girls in education, because she believes that every girl should have the chance to shape her own destiny – just as Michelle has done!

MICHELLE

Michelle is a big music fan — she especially loves Stevie Wonder

Even though she is a super busy lady, she always makes sure she has time to hang out with her daughters, her husband, and her friends

She adores dogs — alongside Bo and Sunny her childhood dog was called Rex and lived with her Grandad

Michelle eats very healthily ... but loves French fries!

Michelle is the first African American First Lady of the United States

She is a fashion icon! Michelle always looks very glamourous.

She's very funny and super-friendly!

Michelle exercises a lot, and even learns to kickbox! Her favourite sport is tennis

Her favourite colour is lavender

Michelle loves hugs!

She's written two books: *American Grown* and *Becoming*

The Fantastically FEMiNist Michelle Obama

Michelle Obama is such a brilliant, strong, determined feminist figure because she is never afraid to stand up for what she is passionate about. She firmly believes in education, equality for all, and that everyone should be able to follow their dreams. And she never stops fighting to make these things happen!

When she was young, her mum and dad taught her to work hard, laugh lots and help others. She learnt that these three things could support her to do anything she put her mind to! And this is how she lives her life every day. She uses these ideals to fight for others who are less fortunate than her.

Michelle is passionate about building a more equal world. She is determined that everyone should have the same opportunities no matter who they are, where they are from, what they look like, or who they love.

Although she wants fairness for everybody, Michelle is particularly dedicated to helping women. She encourages women and girls to stand up for themselves, to stand up for each other, and to stand up for justice for everyone. And that is exactly how Michelle leads her life!

Michelle believes that you can be anything you put your mind to. And you can be more than one thing. She leads by example: she's a super-clever lawyer, a loving mother, a healthy eating campaigner, fitness fanatic, an enthusiastic gardener, a pianist, a style icon, an activist and a First Lady! She is strong and outspoken, but she doesn't take herself too seriously and is happy being silly, joking on television shows, dancing and rapping.

She wants to make sure that young people everywhere know that they can be whatever they want to be, and believes that education is very important to this. In her final speech as First Lady in 2017, she said:

"I want our young people to know that they matter, that they belong. So don't be afraid … Be focused. Be determined. Be hopeful. Be empowered. Lead by example with hope, never fear. And know that I will be with you, rooting for you and working to support you for the rest of my life."

Encouraging young people everywhere to stay in education, work hard, and fulfil their dreams, she is able to use herself as an example. She came from a poor family, her parents didn't stay in education, and her teachers didn't think she'd manage to get into such a good university. But with hard work, willpower,

and refusing to take no for an answer, Michelle built an amazing life which led her to where she is today. And she uses her own success to help others. She encourages young people to try their hardest, to not be afraid to fail, to help those around them.

Her unwavering determination to encourage everyone to pursue education, follow their dreams, and stand up for themselves is truly inspiring. She never stops giving up her time to support others. Who knows what fantastically feminist feat Michelle Obama will achieve next?

For Karina and Emma x
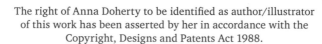

First published in Great Britain in 2019 by Wren & Rook

HB ISBN: 978 1 5263 6109 7
PB ISBN: 978 1 5263 6110 3
E-book ISBN: 978 1 5263 6111 0
1 3 5 7 9 10 8 6 4 2

MIX
Paper from
responsible sources
FSC
www.fsc.org
FSC® C104740

Wren & Rook
An imprint of
Hachette Children's Group
Part of Hodder & Stoughton
Carmelite House
50 Victoria Embankment
London EC4Y 0DZ

An Hachette UK Company
www.hachette.co.uk
www.hachettechildrens.co.uk

Printed in China